ANCHOR
BOOKS

# *ANOTHER DAY IN PARADISE*

Edited by

Chiara Cervasio

First published in Great Britain in 2004 by
ANCHOR BOOKS
Remus House,
Coltsfoot Drive,
Peterborough, PE2 9JX
Telephone (01733) 898102



SB ISBN 1 84418 304 1

# *Foreword*

Anchor Books is a small press, established in 1992, with the aim of promoting readable poetry to as wide an audience as possible.

We hope to establish an outlet for writers of poetry who may have struggled to see their work in print.

The poems presented here have been selected from many entries, and as always editing proved to be a difficult task.

I trust this selection will delight and please the authors and all those who enjoy reading poetry.

Chiara Cervasio
Editor

# *CONTENTS*

## Fine Fellow

He slips silently beneath the wire netting,
stopping to shake dry dust from his coat.
He moves swiftly, then pauses to sniff.
Satisfied, he circles to scent mark,
in the fading light, where there is no bay
to send him packing.

He sits below my window, senses alert,
ermine tipped ears swivelling
to amplify the slightest sound.
Rested, he steps light as air
across a carpet of fallen leaves;
a heavy scent left hanging on the twilight.

***Anita Richards***

## THE JOYS OF SPRING

The snowdrop comes, the daffodil and primrose,
The cuckoo pipes - and spring is here again!
The leaves are getting greener in the hedgerows
And celandines appear all down the lane.
The blossom's bursting forth upon the fruit trees,
The little lambs show spring's a time for birth,
While birds build nests, find mates and raise their families
And life breaks out anew upon the earth.

Our Father, God, in giving us the seasons,
Gave continuity to the human mind.
I like spring for a multitude of reasons.
It brings life, helps the leaflets to unwind
And if it's here, summer's not far behind!

***Jillian Mounter***

## AUTUMN

Autumn glory is back once more,
Summer dreams now slipping away.
Splendid leaves of red and gold
Falling and dancing, then whipped astray.
The sun shines through to show its beauty,
Trees stand graceful and tall.
The breeze lifts the leaves like spinning tops,
The colour and beauty surpasses all.

***Joan D Bailey***

## CHANGING SEASONS

Scenery in the countryside
Changes, four times a year,
From rain, wind and snow,
To days, when skies are clear.

*Springtime,* is the time
When bulbs burst, through the ground,
Also birds start building nests
And little lambs, run around.

*Summertime,* brings sunshine,
When children, love to play
On swings, or in their gardens,
With their playmates, every day.

*Autumn* means, leaves change colour,
Before they fall, from the trees
And the winds, are a lot colder,
Than the summer breeze.

Gales, thunder and snowstorms
Mean that *wintertime,* is here,
So the countryside, looks different
For the fourth time, every year.

***Jean Hendrie***

## Life's Picture

Think of a world that is black and white
Think of a world without any light
Think of a world without any love
Think of a world with no Heaven above
Now look around and don't take for granted
All of the flowers so carefully planted
All of the birds singing in the trees
The rabbits hopping and the humming bees
Beautiful colours: red, yellow, orange, blue
The evening mist, the morning dew
All of these things and so much more
Are there for us if we just open the door
So use your eyes and look around
All that is lost can also be found
So if you wonder what life is about
Just open the window and have a look out
So whether it's raining, sun or snow
These beautiful things are free you know
So spare a thought for those with no sight
Where every day is black as night
Don't waste the gift of sight you were given
Make every day a day worth living.

***Brenda Bartlett***

## September

Last days of September
The nights are drawing nigh
Soon the glowing orange sun
Will vanish from the sky

Mornings bring the mist on high
And grasses wet with dew
Once the distant hills were seen
Now vanished from our view

Soon it lifts and there you'll see
The trees dressed in their robes
Of olive green and yellows
Their autumnal leafy clothes

Summer glory, gone from sight
Next, autumn's leafy glow
Then the winter, in its garb
Of blizzards, ice and snow.

***Beryl Smyter***

## ATTACK

Angry waves that roar and crash,
assaulting rocks, abruptly splash.
Suffocating things in their way,
then roll back on the beach, they lay.
Silently, waiting dormant till
relations rush over and violently spill.
Spray of water, lathering foam,
carelessly rolling, the ocean they roam.

*Nicola Jayne Green*

## FEATHERED FRIENDS

How can it be that such sweet sound
    Comes from so small a bird
While many larger creatures
    Are scarcely ever heard?

Have you watched them bill and coo
    As they sit in their tree?
I'm sure they know happiness,
    Just like you and me.

Have you watched a bird in flight
    While flying in a gale?
Instant flight corrections
    With flying wing and tail.

Some birds will fly a thousand miles
    To lands of warmer clime,
Then fly back here in the spring
    Arriving right on time.

No flight control or radar
    To help them on their way
Their tiny wings keep beating
    As they fly day by day.

God's nature all around us,
    Some common, some are rare,
All need food, protection,
    They all deserve our care.

***Bryan Park***

## A Heron

Yonder on the craggy rock
A heron stands quite still
Watching as the waves chase by
With seagulls screeching shrill

Elegant in grey he blends
Into the shoreline scene
Fishing for his breakfast
Looking regal and serene

Quick and silent, ne'er a splash
He dips his head below
The chilly waters that reveal
A Piscean tableaux

High into the air he lifts
His catch between his beak
Across the sky he flies away
So noble, proud and sleek.

***Kim Montia***

## Our World Of Beauty

Our world of beauty has been made by God,
Wild flowers are springing up through the sod,
Myriad colours doth cover the grass,
In the valleys and on the mountain pass.

And all around us are beautiful trees,
The boughs, covered in leaves, wave in the breeze,
There is copper, apple green and silver,
In woodland, coppice and by the river.

Our world of beauty has been made by God,
The blossom bursts forth as on Aaron's rod,
And bright coloured roses with sweet perfume,
Are woven together as on a loom.

And all around us are beautiful trees,
And every prospect the eye does please,
Fair flowers in the meadow that blend their hue,
Are moistened by the early morning dew.

Our world of beauty has been made by God,
And many harebells in the woods do nod,
We can hear the tinkle of music sweet,
There, where they are clustered beneath our feet.

***Ruth Dewhirst***

## PEACEFUL NATURE . . .

The song of the nightingale,
The hum of the trees,
The sway of the flowers
In the gentle breeze.

The horse in the field,
Running swiftly around,
Feeling full of happiness,
So enchanting, and sound.

I see in the distance,
Way up on the hill,
A beautiful castle,
It stands proud and so still.

When God made this Earth
For us all to live,
He gave nature its beauty,
And a reason to live.

Our dear Mother Nature
Will always be there,
And in the hands of God's will,
To stay loving and care.

We have but one chance,
A day at a time,
Love life and be happy
Until eternal divine!

***Janet Brook***

## WINTER

Leafless trees hang over frozen streams,
Summer memories are but distant dreams.
The cruel winds cut, and to the marrow chill,
Ice forms inside the window and on the sill.

Some lucky creatures in hibernation sleep,
While frozen willows just stand and weep.
Man and beast shelter and warmth do crave,
As the cold hastens the weakest to their grave.

In the midst of this gloom and darkened skies,
A bright star appeared to gladden sad eyes.
We celebrate Christ's birth and we eat and sing,
There comes new hope, and promise of spring.

***John Mitchell***

## THE NEW FOREST

The tranquil beauty
Of this regal forest
Laden with imposing trees,
Ponies to roam as they please!
Packed canopies of golden ferns
Where deer may travel freely
Despite unseen boggy ground,
Where horses canter deeply.
With ducks circling gently around,
Floating on the ponds,
Little brooks wander through the woods
And suddenly - a wild boar
Will chase the strollers a bit more.
All the magic of the animals is there,
For us all to see and share.

***Sammy Michael Davis***

## My Blackbird

My blackbird's there each morning,
I wait until he comes,
He hops around the garden
And spots the biscuit crumbs.

He flies onto the table,
There are raisins there to eat,
He enjoys a few and then he flies
Off, with some in his beak.

Potato and a couple of grapes
Are there when he returns,
He also likes to hunt a bit
For insects and juicy worms.

And when he's very thirsty,
Sips water from the birdbath,
Sometimes he loves to splash about,
I watch him and I laugh.

He nibbles on the bacon fat
And often shares the cheese
With Robin Redbreast and other birds,
And a squirrel if you please.

Several blackbirds join him,
They have a little spat,
Then suddenly they fly off,
On the appearance of a cat!

He is missing for a little while,
Then I hear his chirpy song,
He's sitting on the fence again,
Knows his dinner won't be long.

***June Melbourn***

## The Beauty Of God's World

*(Can be sung to the hymn tune 'Repton')*

I thank you Lord, that I can see
The beauty of your world;
I thank you, too, that I can see
Your love and kindness, shown to me
And to the whole wide world.

I thank you Lord, that I can feel,
Can feel your love to me;
Your love which all transgressions heal,
When we before your throne just kneel
And pray, 'Lord set us free.'

I thank you Lord, that I can hear,
Can hear your words of love,
I know that I should have no fear,
Because you hold our lives most dear
And guide us from above.

Lord, help us now, and every day,
To see your loving care,
And help us feel your touch, we pray,
And hear you guide us in the way;
Oh, Lord, make us aware.

***Anne Gray***

## SPRINGTIME

Would you like to stroll with me along a country lane?
No need for your umbrella, I don't think it will rain.
Mornings are much brighter now, the breeze is not so cold,
The sun peeps out so brightly, around the clouds unfold.

Look at all those little buds spreading everywhere,
The hedgerow is so pretty, a splash of colour here and there.
Over in the meadow, the baby lambs are out,
Not moving far from Mother, they love to prance about.

Daffodils are blooming, dancing with the grass,
It's amazing how they multiply, growing in a mass.
Birds are singing sweetly, perched upon a bough,
The fresh smell of the springtime is really with us now.

A time of new beginnings, the start of life anew,
Eggs are waiting to be hatched, how many? One or two.
Horses in a field of green, feeding on fresh hay,
A blanket covers over them, but I see their dapple-grey.

Miles of different shades to view, a perfect patchwork quilt,
In yonder distance I can see a shed for cows, just built.
The farmer has been busy, ploughing acres since the dawn,
Driving his big tractor, planting lots of corn.

Look there is a duck pond, hens and chickens too,
Across the hedge I hear a noise, what's the hullabaloo?
A pigsty full of piglets waiting for some food,
Mother looks on patiently, her hungry little brood.

Just around the corner, a tree has fallen down,
A piece of log is lying there, bark of rustic brown,
Let's sit for just a moment, reflecting all the view,
How everything's so beautiful, fresh and very new.

Time to stroll back homewards, leaving nature to its chores,
I'm glad the springtime keeper, has opened up its doors.

***Betty Hattersley***

## NATURE

Springtime brings the catkins, lambs' tails of dripping gold
Dangling in the hedgerow, they're pretty and they're bold,
Despite the gusts of winter as yet not gone away
The lovely little catkins are here, and here to stay.

Springtime bulbs protruding, their heads come into view,
Daffodils and crocus will soon be poking through
Brightening the gardens, a pleasure for all to see,
Not everyone will notice, but they will be seen by me.

Seasons ever changing, summer brings the berries,
Fruits of every flavour, my favourites are cherries.
Can you spot the acorns or the conkers when they're due,
Or the lovely little coltsfoot, or the toadstools in the dew?

Skeins of geese, all honking, flying up so high,
I wonder where they're going when they fly across the sky.
Watching tufts of thistledown, blown upon the breeze
And the delicacy of hoar frost when it's frosted on the leaves.

I don't live by farmland, so spring lambs come and go,
And what happens to mountain water, I'm afraid I'll never know.
I think, to hear the gurgling streams run down a mountainside,
Mingled with the sound of lambs before they run and hide.

Perception and imagination, a memory, and our sight
Creates upon the inward eye a vision in the light.
Nature heralds everything, it's there for us all to see,
I'm always very grateful that nature shares with me.

***Linda Cooper***

## SPIDER LACE

It is the beauty of spider webs
In this September as summer ebbs.
Intricate, woven, delicate lace
Beautifully hanging there in place.
The wonders of nature there to see
To think how this could really be.
Twinkling with the morning dew
More wonderful sights are few.
Jewelled droplets fall to the ground
It's Aladdin's cave that I have found.
Sparkling lace from bushes and trees
Swaying so gently in the breeze.
The sun now casts another spell
Such beauty now is hard to tell.
All is glowing in the sunshine
Garden now is a diamond mine.
Colours flashing all around
Fallen leaves the only sound,
As they race over the ground.
I marvel at the beauty I see
As all the colours flash for me.
A tiny spider spins its lace
My garden becomes a magic place.
Now I walk with great care
As not to destroy a spider lair.
Nor must I break the spell
Of this beauty in rhyme I tell.

***Mary Long***

## Here Is Home

Time stands still at the top of the hill,
As I look down on the valley so fertile and green.
Home is down there in amongst that pretty scene,
Where silence is so complete, that it gives you a chill.

The brook gurgles as it runs past the house,
You can see the fish jumping in water so clear.
Through the grass and trees, you can see rabbit and deer,
To see them quite clearly, be quiet as a mouse.

At night, you can hear all the natural sounds,
The animals and birds, their joy knows no bounds.
You feel cosy and warm in your comfy bed,
Close your eyes, my love, rest your weary head.

***Helen Trevatt***

## A Peaceful Scene

This peaceful scene
The beautiful white house
Benevolently beaming on the grounds there below
Its reflections a-shimmering with the fishes a-swimming
In the pool far below
They dart in and out, imaginary windows
Like pools of shimmering light
The sun is a-shining on this summer's day
The birds in the trees they are a-singing
As they look for food to feed their hungry brood
The bees are a-buzzing
Pollen they are collecting for their winter needs
Butterflies are basking in the summer sun
What a beautiful place to be!
All is at peace,
No screeching of brakes
No noise of drilling
No noise to spoil my day
Just the gentle drone of a motor far away,
So I just sit and dream
In this peaceful scene
An oasis in this day and age.

***Patricia Turner***

## THE SKYLARK

It's a still, still common
Lying in the heat,
When from the deep-sleep silence
A voice rings clear and sweet.

It's a gay, brave skylark
Rising to the sun,
To the bright, light sky
Her flight is begun.

What a clear bird shape
Soars above the hill!
What a star-like speck
Is ascending still!

What a song-long way
That little bird has flown!
From what a sky-high height
To dive down lone!

That clear, pure voice
Is singing again.
I hear it long, long after
My childhood's refrain!

***Jacqueline Ives***

## AUCHNAFEE

Here amid the hills are we,
Along the road to Auchnafee.
Here there's quiet and solitude,
Away from throng and multitude.
Here the water ripples by,
Buzzard soars up in the sky.
Here you'll see the deer come down,
You'll see rabbits - black and brown.
A colony of owls live here,
And eagles hunt - or so I hear.
Here is nature at its best,
The heart feels easy - soul at rest.
Accept the sound of shot you hear,
Man - with all his faults - is also here.

Here in Auchnafee again,
To see this place in pouring rain.
Still the magic doesn't fail,
Despite the lightning, thunder, hail.
The waterfalls come tumbling down,
Boiling streams to chocolate-brown.
Then suddenly the storm is still,
Soft sunlight touches distant hill,
In silhouette against the sky,
A herd of deer to please the eye.
God willing, I'll come here again,
In sun or mist, in snow or rain,
Where feet - and spirit - can roam free,
Here in lovely Auchnafee.

***Sylvia Fox***

## Late August

Now sleeps the daffodil and primrose wild
Beneath the turf so sell warmed by the sun,
And bracken climbing through the blackthorn hedge
Cast broadest fronds above the wild plum.
And all the cornfields look so brown and sere
Where combines cut and harvested the wheat,
To leave huge rolls of straw in bundles bound
For use by cattle through the winter deep.
A hush descends on each departing day
Where orchards glow with golden ripening fruit
And luscious grapes along the vineyard wires
Will make rich wine from all the sweetened juice.
Each wood and hedge is clothed in deepest green
Where crickets chirp their high-pitched roundelay,
And swallows gather on the cable wires
To tell us all they soon must fly away.
Now flaunts the trumpet flowers of pure white
Above the luscious fruit of bramble briars,
Where stands a feast for all the autumn birds,
Or us to take, if this be our desire.
The thistledown that floats on balmy air
Give promise to a season yet unborn,
And on the lush green grass around my feet
Are crowns of jewels, every waking morn.
Now, from my cottage window looking west
I watch the sun move southward day by day,
And all too soon these precious hours will pass
As autumn storms are not too far away.

***John Wilson Smith***

## POEM FOR NEW YORK

Brooklyn wondered,
'Where are the stars?'
As the forgotten figure
Cast its sight upwards.

'Maybe someone has taken them away
They all shone so brightly
The lights of a thousand souls
I still think of them today.'

Brooklyn's eyes they widened
And tried to make some out
But Brooklyn found nothing was there
Not a single speck around.

'Oh Empire can you see some?
I so look up to you
Use your height and tell me
That the stars are there by you.'

'Brooklyn don't you worry
I'm sure they're not so far
Though I haven't seen them either
But be sure that stars there are.'

'Liberty are there some by you?'
'Hello Brooklyn, look around
The torch I hold is still well lit
And the stars are safe and sound.

If you have faith, look up now
Through the clouds are bits of sky
And the stars are there, some shining through
Brooklyn see, they're still all right!'

‘Oh Liberty, oh Empire too
They’re there still, can you see?
Though I can’t see the constellations
But that’s good enough for me.

I can now look to tomorrow
For brighter days will come
Though I won’t forget these lessons
And how I thought the stars had gone.’

***Daren Leonard***

## FAIRIES' DISGUISE

You'd think you were watching a fairy ball,
When colourful butterflies come to call.
It's the magic of their dance,
That seems to hold you in a trance.

Such beauty on display,
One could watch them all day.
The red admiral took command,
All the others were also grand.

Some gracefully in the sun lay,
Whilst others around flowers play.
A buddleia gives them showers,
From the water she catches in her flowers.

They must be fairies in disguise,
Drinking where the water lies.
They seem to love red, mauve and blue,
And will venture on something new.

From flowers they have nothing to fear,
It's the sprays they have to keep clear.
Buddleia bushes they love the best,
Some gardeners say they are a pest.

***Margaret Upson***

## A Drawn Curtain

When the sun slides up the morning sky,
Singeing, tinging the clouds
With soft fingers of light,
Stroking away the last traces of night,
I watch the first faint blush
Stealing across the face of Heaven, the flush
Of daylight dawning
On a still-sleeping world.

I hear the chorus of the dawn -
The choir of nature -
Heralding the birth of the new day,
A perfect anthem, song, hymn, roundelay
That bends and breaks
The night's black branches
As surely as a hand
Draws back a curtain.

With that first early flooding light
The trees awaken, dangling
Silver spangles from their finger-ends
Like some sequinned circus star,
And on the far horizon
A golden ribbon
Ties the sea to Heaven.

***Betty McIlroy***

## SUMMER BREEZE

*(After a painting by Tom Browning)*

The cliff-top breeze sang in my ears,
The sky was amethyst above,
And drifting cloudlets shed like tears
Their sweet epiphanies of love.

The sun-ripe landscape seemed to glow
With strange intensity of hue,
And radiant blossoms fell like snow,
As if to make the world anew.

And suddenly your face was there,
Whose darkly enigmatic eyes
Made music of the sighing air,
And raptures of the steepled skies.

You sauntered on the sheep-cropped downs
Through little heavens of wayside flowers,
And silent hills with wooded crowns
Kept vigil through the dreaming hours.

And far away, the planished sea
Gleamed silver in the morning sun,
And sanctified your memory
To savour when your hour was done.

And so you went your endless way
Unhindered, to be seen no more,
Yet still your spirit sings today
From heart to heart, and shore to shore.

***S H Smith***

## AN AUTUMN STROLL

The autumn sunshine sinks down low and
Crisp leaves crunch beneath my feet.
A tractor is busy in the field
And the air smells damp and sweet.
Horse chestnuts are falling to the ground in the breeze
And rooks are squawking high up in the trees,
Pheasants stroll idly across the country lanes,
The clip-clop of horses with riders holding their reins.
Then a squirrel pops his head out from behind a large oak tree,
He jumps from branch to branch, getting further away from me,
When suddenly a deer appears from nowhere, looking quite aloof,
And birds parade in line on the village church roof.
I'm going home again now, I've seen some lovely sights,
But I'll be back this way again, as it's been just sheer delight.

***Hazell Dennison***

## Misty Morning

Through the mist
The trees appear,
Grasping branches
Jump out near,
The mighty trunks
Reach so high,
Stretching up
To touch the sky,
Where vapours merge
Into atmosphere,
The sun bursts through
Then all is clear.

***Gilly Jones-Croft***

## Be With Me

Be with me,
    Where the wind blows free,
        High on the mountains,
            Or out on the sea.

Be with me,
    Where the flowers are sweet,
        With no fancy trappings,
            Just the grass at our feet.

Be with me,
    Where the seabirds soar,
        Feel the salty spray,
            Hear the waves crash the shore.

Be with me,
    Let's dance and flow,
        To such beautiful places,
            Let us go.

***Carol Ann Darling***

## ODE TO ENGLAND

England, oh England, the land of my birth,
You are the most beautiful country on Earth.
With plenty of green, pleasant land to be seen,
The same over generations as it has always been.

Living in rural Devon I'm bursting with pride,
There is plenty of farmland and lots more beside.
In the fields there are horses, sheep and cows,
So calm and peaceful, I can watch them for hours.

Then there are the towns with seaside beaches,
With awesome views I'm rendered speechless.
Hills and moor covered with gorse and heather,
That still look impressive whatever the weather.

With red evening sunsets that give a bright glow,
I love the splendid colours in a double rainbow.
We have castles and stately homes by the score,
Silently waiting for people to come and explore.

All this beauty around me strikes a chord,
There really is no need to holiday abroad.
So many interesting places to visit right here,
England, oh England, you deserve a big cheer!

***Rosemary Davies***

## When The Sun Plays

The sun has finally risen, and it's coming out to play,
Sunglasses tucked behind its ears, heading down our way.
Sunbeams all dancing happily, rays surfing in the sea,
Warming up the sand to welcome you and me.

A warm breeze joins the sun at play, and gently moves the sand,
To help the little sunbeams, with their buckets in their hands,
The rays have finished surfing, and swim amongst the waves,
Whilst all the little sunbeams build their castles with their spades.

Then on the beach they settle, to bask in Mother Sun,
Who shines upon their castles, highlighting every one
Until she tells them time to go, they gather up their spades,
The rays a final surfing game, among the growing waves.

Then off come the sun's sunglasses, as she gathers in the rays,
The little beams now weary, carry home buckets and spades,
To settle in their mother's arms, as the sunlight slowly fades,
To dream about the fun they had, amongst the dancing waves.

***K Townsley***

## Sparrows

People say they are common,
Just a tiny little pest.
Yes! They are quite common,
But they fly around with zest.
You find them merely dull,
Just ordinary brown?
They're really far from dull,
Just watch them flutter down.
No two alike, their feathers shade
From light to warm, dark hue.
Each bird is clad in autumn's shade
And sprinkled with the dew.
Can you imagine seasons
No cheeky sparrows round?
I can't imagine seasons
Without their chirpy sound!

***E Balmain***

## The Rainbow Abides

Red - like sunset or apples sweet
Or embers glowing or desire when we meet -
That is the warmest colour of them all.

Orange - like wallflowers in the spring
Or juicy, cooling fruit or the afterglow in evening -
That is the most comforting colour of them all.

Yellow - like summer sunshine or crocuses
Or bananas in bunches or elation as it on love us focuses -
That is the cheeriest colour of them all.

Green - like fields or trees or valleys or smooth hills
Or rivers as summer with beauty each day fills -
That is the most soothing colour of them all.

Blue - like distant mountains or the cloudless sky eternal
Or the restless sea or the bluebells under trees in bright days vernal -
That is the most peaceful colour of them all.

Indigo - like stormy clouds or wintry skies at dusk
Or shadows or when happiness has gone leaving only memory's husk -
That is the dullest, dreariest colour of them all.

Violet - like shy violets or grapes or royal velvet
Or mourning or sins' true forgiveness to the soul well-met -
That is the richest, most regal colour of them all.

We see them all as the rain subsides
And the sun shines out and the rainbow abides
Over land and sea for just a short while -
We see them all and they make us smile!
And together, thus, they make it appear, awhile,
That life's not so bad, after all!

***S V Batten***

## ENVIRONMENT, ENVIRONMENT

E volution started life so grand
N ations of being form from the land
V alleys, mountains, trees and sea
I lluminate the heavens, the stars can be seen
R adiant the colours of the rainbow beam
O zone is trying to protect the human race
N ature is disappearing with great haste
M ankind must do something to save further generations
E nergy must save sooner than later
N arrate this poem to one and all
T ime is getting shorter, act now before we fall

E volution from the beginning of time
N ew life form of every kind
V ision of a clean new Earth
I deal example of new birth
R iver and sea now turning brown
O zone above with broken cloud greatens
N ations must help each nation
M ankind must all stop being made
E nergy to save we must nag
N AG is the solution
T he dirtiest word is pollution.

***P Brewer***

## NERJA CAVES

The southern coast of Spain can boast a wondrous sight,
Where the ancient Nerja caves present their glory.
Mystical, magical, haunting as night,
In 1959 they did reveal their glory.

Cavemen, dwellers of twenty thousand years ago,
Left wall paintings, artefacts, bones,
For future generations to discover, and show
How they lived, in primitive homes.

Columns, stretching majestically, up to the rooftop high,
Stalagmites and stalactites, formed from ancient time,
Water dripping from above, yet below the ground is dry,
Mother Nature's miracle, a vision, so sublime.

The ever-curious tourist will visit, on vacation.
For man, he likes to gaze in wonderment.
Singles and families, visitors from many nations
Will say, 'Such as this is heaven-sent.'

Hidden lights reveal, in murkiest recess,
Strange resemblances to man and beast.
A dog, a monk, small child in national dress,
Ponder and with receptive eyes absorb this feast.

In looking, speechless do I behold perfection,
Nature's sculpture, with guidance from God's hand,
Humbled by the stillness, convinced that this erection
Reaches out beyond the realm of earthbound man.

***Pamela Carder***

## Listen, Quiet Heart

Listen, quiet heart.
October comes again.
Birds will soon be
carolling the rain.
Poets will walk
A gold leaf road,
chrysanthemums make
them think of God.

***Marion Schoeberlein***

## CHOPPY

It's a very choppy changing day, weather hot then cold,
One-minute sun, two hours rain and then clouds do come
Makes me think about my life, for that's the way it's been
Like the change of seasons, you all know what I mean.

First you're up above cloud nine, a lovely place to be
Where everything is magic, in this world you're fancy free
To do everything you want to, even fly to kingdom come
The world is now your oyster, and the pearl that you have won.

Years will pass, with changing scenes, battles to overcome
Brought back down to earth, to fight them every one
Sometimes you win, sometimes you lose, that's the way it is.
Keep searching for the rainbow, to let the sunshine in.

Still we look for reasons, why some things have to be.
'It's really not for us to know,' says, ever-searching me.
Just be content, I tell myself you've been there at the top
My life's been one adventure, my journey's nearly stopped,

The best is really still to come, like the flower follows seed
Such wondrous things may come about, all could be revealed
Now is not the time to mope, just pray and do what's right
The answer is approaching, could be this very night!

***Joan Prentice***

## Lady In Waiting

Oh infant year conceived in the snow
Tentatively watching the way you will grow
Blossoming gradually into spring
Seeing the new life that you will bring

When fully weaned the summer arrives
Encompassing all that you once magnified
Thawing the Earth with its warmth
Shrivelling streams when reaching extremes
But slowly subsiding with autumn arriving

Maturing gracefully with golden hues
Thinning out warmth as the year ensues
Being replaced with a wintry feel
But the beauty of frost has its appeal
Glistening, sparkling all around
Almost fully grown the year now abounds

To complete the cycle, laying the snow
Grand lady winter has not far to go
Before, once more, conception takes place
For the future spring
Thus setting in motion new life once again.

***Dawn Sansum***

## HALFWAY THERE

Can you hear screeching monkeys and the squawking macaws,
or see the flutter of butterflies in bright array?
Can you hear gurgling streams or the shower of waterfalls?
Turn your face to feel the heat of the sun at midday.

A gentle rustle in the undergrowth on the forest floor,
then a crack of twigs as a snake slides easily by.
You can stand in awe at the trees stretching tall,
their canopy of branches make light flicker from the sky.

Close your eyes and imagine the feeling
of a solitary raindrop on your hot skin, till
another and another in quick succession bring
the torrential rain to soak and thrill.

Can you hear these sounds or picture the sight
of life unravelling with no urgent care?
Within the magic of the rainforest, both day and night,
close your eyes to imagine, you'll be halfway there!

***Tracey Lynn Birchall***

## SPRINGTIME

As I sit down by the riverside
Watching two swans glide side by side
The pond was smooth, and so very clear
Reflections of the swans, came quite near

Watching the ducks, with their little offspring
Wading in the pond with their six ducklings
Leading them cautiously towards the land
Guiding them carefully, as God had planned

Onto the waters again they did float
With beautiful feathers, and waxen coat
Watching through the peace of the day
As squirrels came out of the willows, to play

One squatted, upon the old oak seat
While, feeding him with nuts, oh what a treat
His paws against his mouth and cute little face
So carefully eating them one by one, at a small pace

The hours I thought, went quickly by
As a pied wagtail flew towards the sky
He sang a sharp twill, a twittering sound
Collecting twigs, feathers and moss on the ground.

Building their nest, in the April sun
Flying back to collect twigs, one by one
Working hard together, with ease
As the wind whistled with a light breeze

When, walking away, in the warmth of springtime
Listening to birds, sing with rime
Such peace was there, so full of bliss
As lovebirds stole, their first kiss

When the day turned, to the shadows of the night
The swans and ducks rest, under the pale moonlight

***Jean P McGovern***

## KALEIDOSCOPE

High in the Heavens
Against a backcloth of azure blue,
The golden orb
Now sprays its curtains of light
The gentle fingers of a zephyr has blown away
The black silk of the night.
Clouds of pink-topped cotton wool
Glide swan-like through the sky stately and slow
Looking with lofty disdain upon the Earth below.
Blossoms of myriad hues dip and sway in waltz time
Like maidens whirling in a stately dance,
Then, through the teeming vegetation,
A rainbow-coloured bird of paradise
Darts in swift flight.
A panoramic spectacle, a feast to the sight,
Kaleidoscope of colour, movement and light.

***Lil Bordessa***

## DEVON SPRING

Winter gardens dull and dreary
Devon starts the season early
First, the snowdrops' pearly cups
Shyly lifting, winged white
Heads bowed low a gentle sight
A fairyland of spring.

Crocus, purple, gold and white
Regal with their heads upright
Blooms in clusters heavenly searching
Under trees on lawns and borders
So pretty in their own disorder
Colour spreading spring.

Grape hyacinth the fruit of flowers
Filling Earth with tiny flowers
Built in layers and layers of bells
Partly hidden by their leaves
Complimented by the trees
Muscaris is the spring.

Gardens carpeted with gold
On red, red earth when weather cold
Joyous, is the narcissus
In grass so green in various shades
Of orange, red and white, till fades
Spirit, rising, spring.

***Betty Mills***

## VIEWPOINT

Looking out from the window beside which I write,
I soon almost forget I'm secure on the ground!
For the dainty green tracery picked out in leaves
Of multiple shades on the trees all around
Draws my eye to its beauty, through which I espy
The far tops of more trees in the valley below,
As I glimpse the green downs on the opposite hill.
All this canopied by vast, magnificent clouds,
Some scudding at speed, while yet others seem still
And just lazily drift in fine fanciful schemes.
Did I say I forget I'm secure on the ground?
Yes, my mind soars the treetops with joy in my heart.
Yet secure I am too, for of course one's secure
When kept by the God who created each part
Of my favourite view - and so much more beside.

***Elma Heath***

## Our Summer Garden

I sit and laze on the garden seat, in the early evening sun,
Still pleasantly very warm, though the day is almost done,
I'm feeling content and proud, of my neat borders and lawn,
As I breathe in assorted floral scents, I try to stifle a yawn,
The wheelbarrow bursts with colours, of oranges and white,
Mimulus, pansies and lobelia, fill the wishing well so bright,

Large containers on the patio slabs, a picture of cream and gold,
Pink petunias in hanging baskets, trailing down as petals unfold,
Birds splashing in the ornamental bath, in-between feeding young,
Climbing ivy mixed with sweet honeysuckle, on the wall is hung,
On the trellis arch around me, flowering clematis are entwined,
Bedding plants cover bases of fuchsias, protecting the roots do find,

The grass edged with marigolds and mauve blue campanula bell,
Healthy buddleia shrubs, full of buds, are looking very well,
Clumps of yellow catmint set off a multi-coloured rockery,
Housing ornate gnomes, rabbits and frogs, making it quite merry,
Delicate asparagus fern grows strong beside the golden rod,
Now reaping rewards of hard work, as I relax and gently nod.

***G Siddall***

## The Allotment

There they all work from morn 'til end
No complaints now about having to bend
Tending the vegetables urging them to grow
No weeds to be seen they just had to go.

With cabbages, cauliflowers, beans and peas
Parsley, celery, beetroot and leeks plenty of these
Lettuce, scallions, onions, some radishes too
Spinach, broccoli, parsnips and carrots grown for you.

Some grow potatoes first to clean up the soil
Thus making the future work less of a toil
While others just devote their ground to flowers
Tending to the blooms for hours and hours.

Allotments are a boon for those in the city
That have no other garden to keep nice and pretty
At either back or front of where they live
And having this patch of ground with time to give.

But whether they plant flowers or vegetables you see
It makes one wonder how it can be
For they are usually all produced from a seed
Urged on by their owners that take such heed.

And as they grow thick as they usually do
They will have to be thinned out this is true
Watered and cared for as they rejoice
Of those vegetables so useful or flowers for choice.

***Imelda Fitzsimons***

## DENISE'S GARDEN

Fragments of Heaven floated down
To claim this as their own,
Marvels of colour and fragrance -
The loveliest I've known.

Pert daisies polka dot the lawns
And white aubrietia sprays
Give lacy borders to the green
Like broderie anglaise.

A banquet of delicious pinks
Entices saffron bees
To serenade the sweetened air
With buzzings on the breeze.

Like an exotic butterfly
The yellow iris poses
With petals poised like wings in flight
Above the scarlet roses.

Powerful sunbeams probe the trees,
Their radiance reaching down
To almond leaves, absorbing light,
Where red enriches brown.

Wind carries soporific sounds
Of rhythmic rippling streams,
Of cooing doves and tinkling chimes
That lull me into dreams.

Here in this beautiful garden
There's magic all around me.
It celebrates what nature is
With beauties that astound me.

***Celia G Thomas***

## The Watcher

My son, Dylan Pugh,
Watched how the wild world grew,
And crawled, and walked, and swam, and flew -
And with each fresh fact, each new clue
A sense of wonder he found, too,
As he watched life itself renew!

***Dan Pugh***

## THE PASSING OF WINTER

Rage while you may you blustering coward -
tread on your spiteful way,
Soon you will hear the trip of spring
with measured step and gay,
Enjoy your spree you whipping wind -
winter's bitter frosty page,
The warming sun will chase you soon
from your glistening icy stage.

In a myriad hides, the forest folk
rest in peaceful shelters deep,
And nature's seeds 'neath covers soft
nestle down to sleep.
Untouched by winter's fretful rage,
they listen with soft sighs,
To slumber in silent patience
until its anger dies.

Soon will come a blushing spring -
a tender loving bride,
Winter's mantle, ripped and torn
is gently put aside,
Eagerly Earth removes his cloak
and clasps in fond embrace,
His radiant virgin partner
with her shyly smiling face.

She yields and nature quickens,
spring is expectant mother now,
Swelling with sweet fruitfulness
which in season will endow
All creatures with the milk of life,
free and by Heaven blest,
Nursing all with a mother's love
at her abundantly flowing breast.

***F R Smith***

## RUSTIC RHONDDA

On the valley floor there were meadows to be seen
Ascending then to pastures green,
Then higher still to the woodlands and ferns
The natural beauty, can but make one yearn,
The brooks and streams to the river run
All catching the gleam of the summer sun,
Along the banks were colourful shrubs
And wool covered tree trunks, where sheep rub,
Stagnant pools where tadpoles are found
With the call of birds, a most pleasant sound,
And drystone walls that the boundaries make
Which is also the home of the local grass snake,
The woodlands too, can hold their own
From leaves so green, to acorns brown,
With beech, oak, fir, all tall and proud
Fighting for light as they reach for the clouds,
As the valley meanders on its way
An occasional farm, with fields of hay,
All this of course, was before my time
Everything has changed, from beauty to grime
The valley is scarred, with old coal tips
And the shortage of jobs is on everyone's lips,
Once colourful and rustic, the Rhondda was great
Alas now, it's been left, to its own fate.

***D Richards***

## NATURE'S BOUNTY

A carpet of velvet green and lush,
So smooth, so soft to the touch,
The breeze drifts across rippling the grass,
Flowers in the border, colours to contrast,
So many species, so close together,
They drink the cold rain and smile at the sun,
Masses of blooms spreading their perfume.

Bees flying busily from flower to flower,
Pink roses blooming in the bower,
Blackbirds on the rooftops whistling to each other,
Wind in the trees like music on the breeze,
Butterflies flitting around the stocks,
Heady scents from the hollyhocks,
A balm to the soul, a garden of peace.

The wind rustles the fronds of the willow tree,
Great branches sweep across the lea,
Small blue tits hang on long nut feeders,
Chattering sparrows follow their leaders,
A robin surveys this scene, bright eyes twinkling,
Water running through the fountain, splashing, tinkling,
A haven of peace, God's own place.

***Elizabeth Hiddleston***

## Red Grass

In winter thereabouts the grass is red
And trees, their summer raiment shed,
Stand in pools of their own gold;
While russet bracken long since dead
Lies along the mountain's fold.

Green colours only where the spruce,
Awaiting harvest and another use,
Stands planted neatly in its forest square.
A contrast to the randomness
Of nature, everywhere.

Then endlessly it seems, the rain
Tap, tap, taps upon the pane.
The days are short, and long the night,
But in the hearth the fire is bright
And now is time to play and sing
Content that after winter . . . spring.

***Richard Stead***

## TREES

As a child I loved to draw -
People, houses, trees.
My trees had a solid brown trunk
Topped by a round green ball
Or else stiff stick-like branches
Jutting out unnaturally.

Growing older, I looked around me,
Really saw the trees.
Such a multitude, all different,
Trunks that were slender
Bending in the wind,
Beautifully patterned bark
Or shining silvery-white of birch,
The solid massive oak
Its trunk all rough and gnarled,
With spreading roots like tentacles.
The glorious green of leaves,
Shade upon shade which in the autumn turned
To flaming russet, red and gold.
A fascination was the shape of leaves,
Slender and trailing, hand-shaped,
Rounded or spiky, sharp to touch.
In wintertime denuded branches
Formed a tracery against the sky
While others flaunted their year-long foliage
Enriching the bare landscape,
Providing shelter for the roosting birds.

***Roma Davies***

## Loch Katrine

Surrounded by beauty
My breath overtook
By a beautiful loch
In the Trossachs I stood

Loch Katrine that was
Her name
With steam ship tooting
Upstream she came

Trees so tall, magnificent
And green
Calling me back sweet
Katrine

I feel the breezes blowing
I hear the young birds sing
I see the river flowing
Onwards into spring

White clouds were forming
As eagles soar up high
Winds forever blowing
Creating patterns in the sky

I'm captured and imprisoned
In this woodland scene
As I hear her call
Sweet Katrine

***Marilyn Davidson***

## Great Land

I look out upon this great land before me
With birds wheeling in the sky
Children playing, laughing and people picnicking
As river boats chug on by

People walking their dogs down by the bank
Families spending time together
It's a wonderful place this world of ours
Especially when we have nice weather!

***Joanne G Castle***

## Winter And Spring

Umbrella clouds scowling
storm forces howling
timid trees bending
nights unending.
Bleak winter assails.

Frozen earth encrusting
creatures all distrusting
heaving seas enraging
ships disengaging.
Stark winter prevails.

Resurrected life spawning
abating winds yawning
fresh greenery asserting
ecology converting.
Joyous spring exultant.

Dawn's chorus greeting
night 'n' day meeting
clear skies revealing
nature's healing.
Hope's spring triumphant.

***William A Mack***

## MOTHER OF A THOUSAND

Folk will find it hard to describe
This real start of our human tribe
For if, like some, the Bible you believe
Then you'll say it's down to Adam and Eve
So will you agree with me
They had just sons who number three
So I wonder about poor Noah's wife
Who the hell did give her life?
As his father Seth was the only one
Who fathered the wife of Noah's sons.
Still I can't seem to get any joy
So what of the ones God did destroy?
Then Sodom and Gomorrah I almost forgot
Where come the people who lived with Lott.
Saved the families of Lott and his brother
So I wonder of his dad and mother.
His two daughters one son each did bring
They of two tribes became their king
I may somehow sound a fool
But you need the tribe if you're to live to rules
If Cain and Seth there were no other
The only woman was Eve, their mother.

***Colin Allsop***

## Rainbow's End

I had searched for years and years all to no avail,
I had been to many countries, around the world I've sailed.
Many times I thought I had found it, alas, it was not true,
Many men would have given up, but that's something I could not do.
I searched all the seashores, the mountains and glades,
But for over fifty years my goal, it did me evade.
Then I did find it my own backyard,
To realise my search was over, I found it very hard.
There it lay in the puddle, its colours all now mixed,
Alas it was not the end of a rainbow, just oil in some water,
I was really sick.

***Don Goodwin***

## THE DEVIL'S BRIDGE

In all three bridges this Welsh gorge to cross,
The first and second of stone, now covered in moss,
The third of steel spans the lower two,
An attraction for visitors there to view.

Two rivers below meet in a mighty rush,
Tumble over rocks in a three hundred foot gush.
Other waterfalls there to be seen
The water cascading fresh and clean.

The first span of stone built so long ago,
In the twelfth century it's told to be so.
To be called The Devil's Bridge,
Perched precariously, ridge to ridge.

Legend says the Devil took the toll,
For those not to pay, he took their soul.
Their mortal bodies thrown below,
To be washed away by the swift flow.

***Alan J Morgan***

## Weeping Willow

Tall and slender,
Elegantly hanging low,
Other trees surrender,
To your ever-swaying bow.

Through daytime in the sunlight,
You're green and enriched with life,
But in the night's darkness,
You're silver, like the blade of a knife.

You dangle over rivers,
Touch the surface, cool,
And your long, dainty fingers,
Send a ripple through the pool.

Your frame is forever mighty,
You dance in wind so strong,
Your lifespan is overwhelming,
As centuries pass you on.

And yet you seem so sad,
Your life is full of sorrow,
A new day brings little joy,
There is no hope for tomorrow.

As days pass you by,
You never think of sleeping,
You sigh with other willows,
Condemned to eternal weeping.

***Lottie Dolby***

## Sounds Of Silence

*(After a family visit to Old Hunstanton in late March)*

The velvet sand lies smooth and glistening
Whilst waves ripple gently on incoming tide
I stand amid the silence listening
To the sounds of nature far and wide.
Stratas of rock paint a picture divine
Of cliffs that are rugged and old
Hear all the sounds and see all the signs
That paint a picture more precious than gold
Ponder awhile and think on these gifts
That nature so richly provides
Ponder awhile and your heart will lift
Your spirit will soar to the skies.

***Maryska Carson***

## NATURE'S BALANCE

Nature's balance is very fair
She gives us a gift, we call the *air*
We breathe out the old, then in with the new
Replenishing the energy in me and you

Nature shows us just how much care
She has for us all, to give us our *air*
This gift she gives is always free
Mother Earth charges, not even a fee

*Air* so clever, so very cute
Mother Nature asks us, 'Please don't pollute'
Enjoy the gift of your fresh *air*
Look after your Earth, show gratitude and care

***Gill Gardner***

## LADY OF NATURE

She wore a live scarab
as a pendant
and a pair of earrings
studded with fireflies.
At first I thought,
*what a cruel thing to do*
then I noticed her fingers
two rings on both hands
each one adorned
with a ladybird
of a different hue
they too seemed poised
on the brink of flying away
a bracelet of plaited elephant hairs
was coiled around her upper arm.
At dusk she strolled in her garden
and I heard her whisper
to the roses and the dahlias
bidding them goodnight
as if each one of them
was a person
then, when the moon appeared,
she said, 'Now my loved ones,
you may all retire,
tomorrow will be another
joyful day for all of us.'
And out flew the scarab, the fireflies
and the ladybirds,
rejoining their abode
among the flowers.

***Albert Russo***

## I REMEMBER

Flowing rivers,
meandering streams,
carrying along
a lot of my dreams.
Hills of purple,
green fields and clover,
reminding me my days
are not yet over.
Distant lands
with so many a sight,
influencing my life
forever with delight.
A house in a suburb
filled with much love
where I will remain
like a symbol
of a dove.

***Marj Busby***

## La Puesta Del Sol (Sunset)

Fading fingers of skeletal daylight reluctantly let slip
The dying embers of a swiftly setting sun.
And the evening prepares to pay homage to the moon.

A warm and gentle soporific zephyr softly communes
With the sleepy, swaying branches of the serenely sighing trees,
And the sun sinks ever nearer to the purple-black horizon.

The fading light is fast-filled with the rush of beating wings
As the birds of the day return to night-time roosts,
They land on branch and twig, and chatter quietly
In reminiscence of the day.

Twilight shadows lengthen, and in the gloaming light
Nature breathes a heavy sigh, and the day retreats,
As all the creatures of the sunlight take refuge from the night.

The ocean swell becomes benign, undulating with a tender rhythm,
Pacific waves play a placid lullaby upon the shoreline,
Their song carried skywards on the breeze.

The last vestiges of eventide are swallowed by the hungry darkness,
The sun gives up its hold upon the day,
And the moon ascends the heavens.

The lunar light casts a pale reflection of the sun on the scene below,
And the quiet hush of night-time exacts its toll upon the day.
The sun has set, the day is done, and tomorrow is yet to be.

***Juan Pablo Jalisco***

## Farewell Grass Roots

Moorland grasses, remote
Hills green, meadows lush
Raindrops embroider woolly coats
Daisies, buttercups, clover blush.

Spring comes yet once more
Little lambs grow, gambol
Time for us to go
Down country lanes to walk, ramble.

See sheep dip, bath day
Woolly coats being washed
Wool cleaned, sheared
For mills, to spin yarn, cloth.

'Twas noisome this morn 'til noon
Sheep herded into lorries, now gone
I hope there's air, water, soon
No fun being trodden on.

In this world of ours
Compassion give to all
Creatures great and small
Kindness ever, cruelty abhor.

Journey to food chains, lunch pack
Cuts, chops, succulent for flavour
Supermarkets, butchers, shelves to stack
Sunday roasts, families to enjoy, savour.

***Ivy Lott***

## WONDERFUL NATURE

Indeed nature is wonderful
Beautiful wild flowers growing
Beautiful, lovely smells
Freshly cut grass, what a lovely smell
The sunset, what a wonderful sight
Just amazing
Wonderful nature, wonderful nature
Clouds in the sky unbelievable
Just amazing
All sizes and shapes
You can make out faces and objects
Just amazing
Indeed, Mother Nature is wonderful
The seaside a marvellous wonder
Seashore, sandy beaches, the sea just wonderful
Wonderful sight, the sea, the tide coming in
The tide going out
Rippling beautiful waves
Nature is wonderful
Shells and seaweed appear on the beach
Nature is wonderful, wonderful nature
Flowers, trees, sea, rivers, clouds
Parks, forests, fields, sunset and sky
All so, so wonderful
Amazing sight, baby lambs in a field
Cows mooing away and grazing
Fresian, black and white
Herefordshire, brown and white
Nature, a wonderful sight of colours
Wonderful smells
Yes indeed, wonderful nature

***David J Hall***

## THE SEAGULL'S CRY

Seagulls glide over ragged cliffs, soaring high on updrafts,
far away from us.
Calling out above the roar and crash of the waves as they slam
against the cliffs and rocks.
Sending up fountains of white water high into the air,
tinting the air with the tang of salt.
Falling back onto the rocks at the bottom of the cliff with a
loud hissing sound.
Then away, draining back into the sea for the next wave to hit.
Seagulls calling to each other, looking for food to feed their young,
perched high on the cliffs.
Floating in the sky like kites with the strings tethered to the ground,
stopping them drifting off.
Hanging, slowly swaying from side to side in the off-shore winds.
Then diving into the sea, in and out in no time, not getting wet
or ruffling their feathers.
Then up again to wait for the next dive, in between the rise and fall
of the waves.
As the power of the waves humble you at the sheer strength of
something which will run through your fingers.
With jagged peaks, caves and inlets carved by the constant pounding
of the sea over thousands of years.
With all it strength and power you feel stimulated by its awesome
splendour and beauty.
On its gentler side, as it laps softly on the shore, with the seagulls
calling on the water's edge.
Sitting on the rocks or a sandy beach on a warm, sunny day with
no worries on your mind.
The soft, gentle sound of the waves lapping and sapping
on the shoreline.
Sending you far away, from where you are to another place and time.
A place and time with happy memories to lose yourself for a while
in your own thoughts.

***Christopher Bean***

## EVENING LAKE

I walk by water
in strange half-light
when swans drift, darkening
and mallards lift
in dimming air
revealed against
the evening sky.

No questions linger,
no trick of light
can hinder or surprise.
Sometimes dense green
leaf or tree, all known
make momentary screen.

Lake-misting grey
landscape obscures
unruffled, unregarded
night's slow fall
and fading sunlight
diminishes all desire.

***Fay Emerson***

## HOLY-WELL, EASTBOURNE

Bracing breeze caressed our cheeks to a
stimulating awareness of its demanding presence.
Inhaling deeply, the sharp freshness of the breeze
filling our lungs with an enthralling freshness
of intensity, to its consoling feeling of well-being.
Our pace quickened to a lively encounter with the southerly
wind, as it encouraged our strides to lengthen.
Catching the domination of the breeze, the sea rolled and
twisted, each wave with resounding force on the awaiting
shingle. Then with a mighty withdrawing rush of water
the sea rolls and twists, pounding with brutal force, as
another wave with the help of the wind breaks onto the
beach, demanding the tide to turn, as the southerly breeze
is carried away with the receding tide . . .

***Lorna Tippett***

## The Polar Sky And Hemisphere

The white and blue polar sky, where a million stars are darkened,
In a landscape of white moving ice, where polar bears protect
their siblings,
Within the polar sky and hemisphere,
Where giant icebergs move accordingly,
Below a blue-ice sky, with snow falling deliberately,
Colossal icebergs collapse terribly, with the sound of thunder,
Underneath the north and south hemisphere,
Where the wooden ship and sail flounder,
Being crushed mercilessly by pack-ice so slowly,
With helpless eyes watching aimlessly,
Adrift the adventurer prays providence,
In isolation, sequestered and remote from civilisation,
Where raw beauty is evident, and the giant black and blue whales swim,
A monster of the deep breaking waves, while shooting the
white waterfall,
Where rubbery seals glide unnoticed, darting bravely down to the
deep ocean floor,
While above, sledge dogs howl and run their course onwards,
Across a barren landscape, where the Eskimo builds his
ice-igloo perfectly,
Dressed in bearskins, like nomads roaming the ice desert forever,
Drilling holes through the cold silvery ice, they spear fish gladly,
In the distance, giant moose graze the steps of cold paradise,
Where the green forest is snow-capped until summer comes,
Where the Arctic night blows her fierce unstoppable cold biting winds,
Around the high mountain ridge, white vapour clouds circulate,
Where the ice fox digs unsuccessfully, dying from cold and hunger,
While the northern stars shoot across the polar skies,
Within the white cold wilderness, the polar sun recedes on the horizon,
While the white hunter trembles, he falls asleep,
Blessed with hypothermia, frostbite claims his fingers and toes,
Now, buried underneath the onslaught of the avalanche,
The long summer never comes, underneath the polar skies.

***James S Cameron***

## At The Water's Edge

The pool portrays the trees
Taking green shapely branches deep below,
I dip my hand, disturb the smooth illusion,
The picture disappears, depth is denied.
Yet real depth, invisible, remains,
Even to drowning.

Still water whispers,
Flowing water sings.
We seek the spring, follow the lively stream,
Float on the widening river
And at last rejoin the sea,
Strong waves of birth and of eternity.

***Ruth Partington***

## FORGIVE AND FORGET

Let us forgive
Like a swimming river
Smoothening pebbles
And sand shells.
Let us forgive
Like a sweet spring
Mirroring the sky blue love
Of the ever busy skies.
Let us forgive
Like the flowing waters
Not perturbed in quest
In search of her prodigal
Let us
. . . forgive.
Let us
. . . forgive.

***Ezenwuba, Uche C***

## WATER-DROPS

The storm is over
and water-drops

spangle
the spider's web
like precious gems

iridescent pearls
perfectly formed.

***Fay Smith***

## INSPIRED BY NATURE AND WELSH GRIST

Shropshire, bordering north Wales
then outing to see the sea beyond;
the haggard and excitement of hills and vales,
a car ride and hiking, such a bond!

Nature's foliage, high, low and all around
making a host of whatever weather;
rivers and streams cascading to ground,
wild, unruly, both mixture and tether.

People of England fly - holiday abroad
unknowing waters - also a foreign language;
Welsh homes circumjacent, almost a friend,
making room for a road, built on a thin flat sandwich

All that's on the level in this countryside,
lakes, mirrors reflecting the beauty around
railways, superb engineering, requiring a longer ride;
the Welsh gened into upheaval, better straight and sound

I'm sorry my country folk, holiday, say,
just step over Wales into advertised vacation;
but my every trip here, a red letter day
each occasion some new, novel animation.

***J R Lucas***

## COUNTRY WALK

If I set out to walk,
some morning clear in spring,
the weather fine;
the bright day soon
would turn around
and bid me shelter
under leaking leaves.

From culverts,
out of ditches,
dripping mud;
from granaries,
from fretting over bones,
from quiet farms
the dogs would race
to question me;

a stranger in their fields.

***Alex Anderson***

## THE PYRENEES ON A MAY DAY

The hairpin winding bends
That climb the mountain peaks
Are nothing when compared to what you find
When leaving car, to go on foot.

For then you hear, see and feel
All of God's wonders aired,
From tiniest flower, to mightiest peak
To depths below and shadow as
Cast by sun and clouds,
That almost ought to leave a sound
When marking mountainside,
Yet silence still prevails
While moving into space again
Losing forever the mark they made.

But still so much to feel, to see, to hear,
Of sun's hot spots or coolest draughty air.
While barest places beautified
With smallest flowers of white
Or even yellow, pink and purple.
Then sound of water, rushing to find the light of day
From Earth's hidden darkest place,
Fresh and pure to give its life
To every beast and place that waits its turn
Along its steep descent.

Then that which words cannot describe
Of silence whispering stillness
Descending all around, then leaving all behind
But taking much within the soul
With effects on other worlds, another day.

***A V R Cracknell***

## DEVASTATION

Fervently we watch the storm's savagery
Intent upon its cleaving
From the heart of life
Yellow maple leaves.

*Louise Mills*

## The Heavens

Worlds tumbling into one another
    Giant planets crashing out their orbits
Huge stars pulling in light from distant reaches
    Wild chunks of rock spilling across the universe
All on a predefined collision course
    Chaos theory personified

That's what I see when I look to the heavens
    Not just little blinking dots of light
I imagine the rawness, the force and the might
    Of all that went into its making
And more

I can hear the silence in which it all transpires
    It saddens me to think no one can hear
An exploding star must look magnificent
    But without sound
It's just a moving series of photographs

Let me hear the roar
    The growl to display the strength
Like a lion calling its domain
    This is mine
Everybody else leave

The scenes I see enfolding before me
    Makes the night seem alive
While the day makes me yawn
    And I feel so deprived
Waiting for the darkness to return

***Mark Stead***

## OBSERVATION OF WINTER

Winter, season of peace
Tired Earth sleeps with her past
Keeping with her the secret
Of life and death
Mouldering leaf, germinating seed
Snow lies thick on deserted fields
Sun tints the ice
And snow crisp earth
Crunches underfoot
A stream flows under an icy cap
Leaving no trace of its passing
On the bank either side
A robin on a frosty twig
Puffs his feathers against the cold
A hedgehog hibernates in a leafy cocoon
The blurred sun dies
The moon shivers
The leaden day escapes into darkness
Only the sudden hoot of a barn owl
Shatters the cold night air
Then silence . . . peace is everywhere

***Cindy Hagger***

## BORN TO BE BEAUTIFUL

And fruits, and flow'rs, on nature's ample lap?
Swift fancy, fir'd, anticipates their growth;
And, while the milky nutriment distils,
Beholds the kinding country colour round.
Thus, all day long, the full-distended clouds . . .
Indulge their genial stores, and well-shower'd earth -
Is deep enrich'd with vegetable life;
Till, in the western sky, the downward sun is . . .
Look out effulgent, from amid the flush in -
Of broken clouds, gay shifting to the beam.
The rapid radiance instantaneous strikes - so sunny . . .
Th' illumin'd mountain; through the forest streams,
Shakes on the floods, and, in a yellow high mist,
For smoking o'er th' interminable plain, within much heat . . .
In twinkling myriad lights the dewy gems will be.
Moist, bright and green, the landscape laughs around.
Full swell the floods: their ev'ry music wakes, so sunny . . .
Mix'd in wild concert, with the warbling brooks . . . by wind,
Increas'd, the distant bleatings of the hills, are alive . . .
And hollow lows responsive from the vales, hot sparks there,
Whence, blending all, the sweeten'd zephyr springs.
Meantime, refracted from yon eastern clouds above,
Bestriding Earth, the grand ethereal bow . . . the sun is out,
Shoots up immense, and ev'ry hue unfolds, within anytime . . .
I fair proportion running from the red, to shine out . . .
To where the violet fades in the sky.
Here, awful spring, the dissolving clouds moving . . .
From, fronting on the sun, thy show'ry prism;
And, to the sage-instructed eye, unfold in good weather -
The various twine of light, by thee disclos'd yellow spot,
From the white mingling maze . . . the sun is shining brightly.

***Viv Lionel Borer***

## TRANSFORMATION

Neglected,
disused;
ruins revel in green.
Luxuriant,
disorderly.
Insect paradise.

The halcyon summer day
kindles a riot of motion.
Foliage-skimming butterflies,
gracefully dancing,
pirouetting;
flashing colour-coded warnings
to unwanted intruders.

Lazily,
amongst the silent clamour,
aristocrats take their rest.
Honey-drawn,
delicately poised on purple panicles;
or wings outstretched,
absorbing sunshine's warmth.

In that precious transience,
whilst the sun transforms
the blizzard of butterfly wings,
the waste-ground conjures
a playground, full
of summer's snowflakes.

***Joy Morton***

## SMILE

Caught in the round world
Between the four seasons
Giving shape to bright clouds
Holds the sky's slow calm horizon
We are drawn skyward into the future.

Through sunshine and warmth
Walking in the woodlands,
Breathing in and breathing out
To enjoy the goodness of spring air
Such a glorious month of May.

It is a glorious morning
And the air is fragrant
With the touch of happy smiling, with golden hue,
Of all our England's mighty skill and force
The heart of ancient woodlands brings peace and prosperity.

***Heather Aspinall***

## THE SEASONS

The wind blows through the treetops, you can hear its moans and sighs,
The leaves fall down like golden snow before your very eyes.
It looks like things are changing, the trees will soon be bare,
But the sun still shines in a sky of blue and there's a freshness to the air.
This golden carpet covers the forest paths and trails,
Crunching beneath your walking boots, a prelude to winter's gales.
When the golden carpet disappears beneath a covering of white,
The sleet, the snow, the iron hard frost, making day as cold as night.
We look outside each morning with hearts so full of dread,
And we scarcely can believe it, that there are better days ahead.
But as we reach the farthest depths, our minds filled with despair,
We feel a change, slowly at first, as the coldness leaves the air.
And in the sky the sun peeps out, begrudgingly at first,
But just a glimpse is all it takes to know we're past the worst.
Then as the moisture lessens and the sun starts getting stronger,
The long dark nights, they reach their end and the days start getting longer.
For the past few months it's looked like a world of monochrome,
But now the colour's all returned, it's been gone but now it's home.
All the flattened yellowed grass begins to reawaken,
The leaves come out upon the trees, they haven't been forsaken.
And so begin the long hot days and the warm and sultry nights,
The days of basking on the beach, the days of flying kites,
Of running carefree through the woods when the land gives of its best,
Alfresco dining, barbecues, as the sun sinks in the west.
To rise again the next new day, slowly from the east,
Until the mid point of the year when the longest day's been reached.
It won't be very long then until change sets in once more,
And the golden time comes round again and the leaves fall to the floor.
The seasons are like a circle, no true beginning, no true end,
Just a steady gradual changing in Mother Nature's blend.

***Alan Wilson***

## SEA SONG

Summer glistens
shoreline shimmers
waves curve
patterns
across silver sand

Thoughts windsurf
free
to ride high
on gulls' wings
until
the mind
is
bright and still

drowned
by the sounds of sea
in
summer sun

***Helen Clarke***

## THE ROBIN

As I sat on a cold wet bench
Wondering if life was worth the bother
Could I face another day?

I sat and watched the people
Rush past with not a smile
Upon their face,
Thinking what to do.

I sat upon a cold wet bench
With tears upon my face.
From the sky a feather floated down
I watched and watched as it fluttered.

It landed on my knee
Pure white and soft to touch
Did he send it to me?
Then as I watched it changed

A sound so soft and gentle
Sounded in my ears

Rare are you to cry such tears
Over pain you have shared
Blinded by so many hurts
In all that you have done
Now is the time to forgive

The song had been sung
I am here to remind you
He never left you dear
I hope you can see

I may be a feather
A robin maybe
A star that you wish upon
Just believe in me.

***R Mills***

## SHE'S ALWAYS RIGHT

Quietness
And grey,
The start of a day.
A cold chill
In the air.
No lightness of song
From bird in a tree.
No sign of the sunshine
Or warmth from its rays.
Black Tuesday,
Why so be?
Whatever is wrong?
The clock ticks
Its seconds
One after one.
The leaves on the branches
Fall in the wind.
A glimmer of light
In the sky.
Then the coo of a dove
Says, 'All is at peace'
And the blackbird
Joins with his call.
The season is turning.
Gathered the harvest.
Now time for reflection
And rest.

***Lyn Sandford***

## Spirit Of The Mountains

Millions of stars in a velvet sky,
Snow-capped mountains reaching high,
A fell of heather at their feet -
My nostrils filled with the scent of peat.

A night owl fluttered overhead -
An eagle with its wings full spread -
And far away the bagpipes sound
Spreading their music all around.

Hiss of the wind through yellow gorse,
River rushing along its course,
Fairies dancing along its bank
Laughing gaily at every prank.

Dawn painted the sky a liquid gold -
What a beauty to behold!
The Lord with His majestic hand
Shaped this country, my native land.

***Mary Baird Hammond***

## A Washing Day

The sun was shining brightly.
Such a beautiful drying day.
I hung my washing on the line,
While my granddaughter and I played.
Suddenly a strong wind blew,
Almost blowing my washing away.
I ran to take it off the line
As quickly as I could,
When suddenly one of the sheets
Wrapped around the swing,
And me, I could not see.
Bang went my knee against the iron bar.
Can you imagine the pain I felt
Dislocating my knee?

***Doreen Petherick Cox***

## JUDGEMENT DAY

They came from the heavens to the Earth
With the power to ravage and burn.
Asteroids and comets; shooting stars
From the outer limits of deep space,
Or the area between Jupiter and Mars,
To fall towards the sun.
But fell into the path of the passing Earth,
These wanton wanderers; fearful destroyers,
Vile things, the planet wreckers.
And great extinction they bring.
Death to dinosaurs and trilobites,
Tiny diatoms and swirling ammonites,
To stop conventional evolution,
Or luck good fortune judged,
What life was to survive,
And thereby opened other doors,
New life forms to grow and explore,
So now we wait.
Will we this time escape?
A remnant on the moon or Mars,
Looking back to the once green Earth,
Contemplating our poor planet's fate.

***Jonathan Pegg***

## PARADISE FOUND

All was well in Plantland, Zazing was in his palace,
the dirt mines were running at full production
and the garden was a beautiful place.
The nurses at the egg factory celebrated another bumper harvest
of baby ants. Sugar flowed from the big house where the humans lived,
and the priest ants at the ear temples enjoyed the status of princes.
There were no female priests; women ants were all nurses.
Would there ever again be such an age as this when all believed
the same thing? With all of Plantland worshipping the ant king, Zazing,
there remained only one task left;
the humans too must be brought under control.
Then indeed, paradise would be found in the ruins of Humania.
Unlike humans, ants never slept and sleep would be the 'crusties'
downfall.

***Vann Scytere***

## The Lovely Autumn Chestnut Tree

Summer has gone, your beauty ever so proud
To see your lovely green display
But now cold winter comes
With your beautiful red and brown, orange and gold
What a beauty to behold
I hold my breath
And watch the sun
As she gives you a shower of gold and brown
You played your part
In spring and summer
Now you are going to rest
But not with shame or loss
Our good Lord has shown you a beauty
This tree
No picture can paint
I cannot grasp the colours
You display
A gift of magic from our Lord
We do stand at this beauty
You can match the rainbow
Any day of your life
Belongs to all
To see the beauty
Of the chestnut tree
You stand so proud
In your winter way.

***M Houseman***

## WINDY RAVES AND AMBER RAYS

Cool winds blowing, stir up Mexican waves and raves!
Heaving beech and sycamore, ash, willow and haw;
Tree limbs thrash out stereophonic sounds,
Rousing snappy bashes to wild breeze, then eases
Down, but swiftly comes roaring, more blasts resounding!
Branch clashing with branch and leaves all tremulous;
A billion rustling kisses send leafy flurries,
Denuding bushes in the surging wind-rush.
Dark clouds gathering pace, billow asunder,
Masking autumn's amber rays here or there;
Spotlights shifting around enliven the thrills.
Yet, a lone kite feathery surfing the currents
Calls eerily; an undeterred predator preys,
Ever scanning with hungry raptorial eyes.
All the while, sunbeams warm lingering
On chilled grass, sweetens sour peat, to steam
And waft an earthy savour ascending.
Tall and thin, rocking and waving seed stalks
Entrance with a shimmying ochre haze.
But wow! The stylish eucalyptus,
Showing off long, swaying python-marked limbs,
Flicker thousands of dazzling jade slivers;
Lanceolate leaves, like shoaling anchovies
Flash-dance silvery in the beaming sky.
A cotoneaster feigns the dress of Christmas.
Adorning her curving arms are glossy beads,
That brightens to a richer scarlet when lit.
Except, it seems discontent to want to see,
Frosted gossamer strands looping as tinsel,
And a snowy dusting of winter's festive show.

***Ramon Gonzalez***

## THE CHOICE

You asked what is my favourite flower
I cannot answer that
    Lest I deny the many blooms
    That grace my garden plot.

For don't you see the artistry
That form the petals round
    The colour and the cup which hold
    The whole bloom from the ground.

The varied hues and shapes abound
With tender loving care
    Appealing to the heart that loves
    The common and the rare.

***R T James***

## LINKS WITH NATURE

Let the voice in the storm
Be your guide
Do not hide,
Let the whispering breeze
Be your friend
Until journey's end.
Let the stars light up your pathway
Tonight and tomorrow too,
Let the sun be the warmth
Inside your heart
Refreshing you anew,
Let the moon be your mentor
Keeping you from errant ways,
Let the rain wash away your sorrow
Bringing you blissful days.

Let the snowfall cherish your love
Share it with everyone,
Let the thunder be your words
Speak them carefully,
Let the trees be your strength
Strong and long-lived,
Let the ocean be your future
Seal your own destiny.

Let the rainbow be your inspiration,
Let all the rivers be your sincerity,
Let the horizon be your fortitude,
Let the blue sky be your dreams,
Let nature be your true spirit,
Reaching out to you, embracing you,
Touching your very soul.

***George S Johnstone***

## Little Brown-Farthing Wren

Little brown-farthing wren
On our garden wall,
Looking down - wondering when
Falling leaves will fall
Hawthorn leaves October,
Poplar, oak and lime;
Now we're in November,
Near the wintertime.

You are so precocious,
First rays of the sun;
We are though - mendacious,
That is why you shun,
Now you're on the pedestal,
Freshly filled with rain,
Carefully you drink your fill,
Grubs you quickly gain;

Little brown-farthing wren,
Smallest I have seen,
Rummaging for food again,
'Ere the cold is keen;
Make our garden home I pray,
Rising with the dawn,
I will look for you each day,
Feeding on our lawn . . .

***Tom Ritchie***

## WINTER

Through the windows sunshine gleaming,
The sky outside is blue,
Looking like glorious summer,
Yet a deceptive view.

The air is cold, the trees are turned,
The clocks are turned back too,
The midnight hour is extended,
A winter crisp and new.

The fallen leaves are freshly down,
Spent not in times long gone,
That's why each season is a first,
Another year moves on.

No time to dwell on errors past,
Future is a stranger,
Arrange to meet it hopefully,
Another chance at last.

***Kathleen M Scatchard***

## COUNTRYSIDE

Somerset where time stands still,
apple picking, tranquillity,
a forgotten world left to folk,
keeping hedgerows, pattern fields,
meadows of poppies, buttercups
country folk did before them.

***Alan Hattersley***

## FISHING

There you sit in the still of the night,
A nice big fish would be such a sight.
These elusive fishes are so sly,
In the dead of night they pass you by.
A quick sly nibble at your bait,
It's oh so cold and getting late.
Nearly time for bed you feel,
Would be nice just to wind in your reel.
Just to feel that fish on your line,
Just a bend in your rod would be just fine.
You awake to the dew upon the grass,
Not one fish the night has past.
Another night, those fish you cannot find,
Maybe next time? Oh, never mind.

***H Scerri***

## This Year's Starlings

gang up in the nearest tree.
They squabble. They fidget.
They noise each other up
behind the turning leaves.

They burst out in little groups,
bunched up and belligerent,
and charge about above the street
screeching defiance at the passers-by.

The whole tree-load explodes shrilly
and shoots off into the air.
They wheel round into the day
claiming it as their own.

They know how to threaten,
to challenge, to antagonise.
Then they batter back into the safety
of failing cover and stiffening twigs.

In the next tree along
I hear the older birds bickering.
They twitter about preserving strength
for the coming winter.

***Stephen Eric Smyth***

## Isle Of Skye

Mighty mountains, misty peaks
Peace and tranquillity we all seek
Sheep grazing on grassy slopes
While man struggles and barely copes
Lochs and rivers clean and free
Reflecting the heavens for all to see
Dolphins dancing in Broadford Bay
Seals basking at the end of the day
God's creation must be protected
Preserved and loved, never neglected.

***Catherine Hislop***